"Mark A. Smith's Guide to Safe, Common Sense Off-Road Driving is published by Cedar Ridge Publishing, P.O. Box 4600, Georgetown, CA 95634. The entire contents are copyrighted and may not be reproduced in whole or in part or in any form whatsoever without the consent of the publisher."

© 2000 Mark A. Smith Off-Roading, Inc.
Revised March 2004, February 2000, January 1997/ Over 60,000 copies printed.

ISBN No. 0-9658763-3-0

INDEX

Introduction 4-5
Be Prepared 6
Safety 7
How To Prepare Your Vehicle 8-9
Thumbs Up 10
Look in All Directions 11
Off-Road Driving Techniques 12

HILLS
Hills 13
Avoid Driving Side Hill 14
Going Up A Steep Hill 15
Going Down A Steep Hill 16
Know Your Angle of Approach and Departure 17
Don't High Center 18

Losing Traction 19

ROUGH COUNTRY DRIVING
Rocks 20-21
Sand 22
Snow, Ice, Dust, Meadows 23
Mud 24
Ruts 25-27
Crossing Streams 28-30
Water Depth 31
Crossing A Log Or Tree 32
Three Point Turns 33-34
Rough Country Driving Summary 35

TIRES
Tires, Tire Pressure 36-37
Goodyear Tires 38-39

INDEX

WINCHING & STRAPPING

Winching	40
Basic, Simple Winching	41
Winching Accessories	42
Using Your Winch	43-44
Large Tree Across The Road	45
Getting Back On The Road	46
Always Use A Tree Strap	47
Snatchum Strap	48-49
Proper Way To Connect Two Straps Together	50
Why We Don't Use Tow Straps With Hooks	51
Winching Summary	52-53
What Winch Do I Personally Recommend	54
What To Take For Off-Highway Trips	55
Road Courtesy	56
Helpful Hints	57
The New "Rubicon" Jeep	58
Off-Highway Road Driving Tips Summary	59-60
The Jeep Jamboree USA Story	61-63
Trail Ratings	64-65
Training Special Forces – U.S. Army	66-67
Los Angeles County Sheriff's Training	68
Expedicion De Las Americas	69-75
Specialized Training	76
Sponsors	77-78
For Sale	79-80
About the Author	81-82

INTRODUCTION

This guide reflects my views and includes tips and techniques learned from more than forty-five years of extensive off-road driving including expeditions and some of the toughest four-wheel drive trails in the world.

A wide variety of off-road situations and techniques are addressed in this guide, including what to do in rough terrain, how to make water crossings, proper hill climbing techniques and effective winching methods. Below are some of the four-wheeling basics which are covered in greater detail elsewhere in this book. They are included here as a quick reminder as well.

Most anyone can successfully drive off-road by simply following basic guidelines and using common sense. Once you have learned the basics, all it takes is practice!

ALWAYS wear your seat belts.

NEVER drink alcoholic beverages and drive.

Do not stand up or allow passengers to stand up in a moving vehicle.

Not all four-wheel drive vehicles or sport utility vehicles (SUVs) are designed for off-road use. KNOW YOUR VEHICLE, ITS LIMITATIONS AND YOUR OWN.

Each 4WD situation presents a challenge. Analyze and examine the obstacle before attempting a difficult situation.

Most rough off-road driving is done at very slow speeds using first gear and low range. When crawling over rocks, speed and power are not necessary. Always drive as slowly as possible. If you have an automatic transmission, gear down to your D1 and D2 range and 4WD Low. Let the vehicle crawl and idle while going over obstacles.

If you see or feel that you are going to need four-wheel drive, put the vehicle into 4WD before you need it. Most 4WD vehicles require a full stop to go into low range. Know your vehicle and how to shift in and out of 4L and 4H. Jeep vehicles must be in neutral in order to shift the transfer case into low range.

INTRODUCTION (continued)

Remember, speed and power are not required. The low gears and low speed of the vehicle idling will generally get you over the obstacle, although it may sometimes be necessary to apply a little throttle when going uphill or a little brake when going downhill.

Another technique we teach for rough off-road driving with a manual transmission is to DRIVE WITHOUT THE CLUTCH! You start and stop the vehicle in gear with both feet on the floor. USE FIRST GEAR AND LOW RANGE, turn the key to start and do not use the throttle. Just let the vehicle start crawling – which it will do automatically with the starter. The engine will start up and idle over the obstacles. If the vehicle stalls, do not use the clutch, just use the starter again. In some cases, it may be necessary to apply a little throttle. You have total vehicle control without the clutch.

(NOTE: Some vehicles may require a manual disconnect in order to drive without the clutch. Please refer to your owner's manual for disconnect information.)

You can drive this way all day and never burn up the clutch and you will not hurt the vehicle driving in this manner. When driving without the clutch in rough terrain you have total vehicle control. An expression we use on the Rubicon Trail is "GITCHERDAMFUTOFFDAKLUTCH". Many times when people drive in rough country crossing over logs, rocks or other obstacles, they have a tendency to ride the clutch. When the vehicle stalls, they push in the clutch and the vehicle will roll back causing them to get stuck or get in trouble. If the vehicle stalls in a critical spot, do not depress the clutch; the starter will generally pull you over the spot.

There is an exception to the above technique; if the vehicle is in a very tight bind or up against a large rock, and if the vehicle cannot move forward through use of the starter, then use the clutch to avoid burning up the starter.

Try to practice this technique before going off-road. Start and stop your vehicle several times **using the key only** – no clutch – no brake – no throttle –WITH BOTH FEET FLAT ON THE FLOOR. Practice this on flat ground.

BE PREPARED!

If you anticipate a 4WD situation, put your vehicle into 4WD BEFORE you get stuck!

You might find it difficult to get the vehicle into 4WD if it is in a bind or stuck. Most 4WD vehicles require a full stop to go into low range. Know your vehicle and how to shift in and out of 4WD-Low and 4WD-High (refer to your owners manual). Remember, 4WD does not mean you always have four wheels turning. Often, in rough terrain, power is shifted to the wheel of least resistance, which means you have one wheel turning in the front and one wheel turning in the back.

Check your vehicle before and after going off-road:

- ✓ Fuel
- ✓ Brakes
- ✓ Oil
- ✓ All other fluids
- ✓ Battery in good condition and properly secured
- ✓ All hoses and belts in good condition
- ✓ Tires in good condition and properly inflated, and a full size spare
- ✓ After being in mud or deep water, it is a good idea to check your differentials and transfer case for water or mud

ALWAYS TREAD LIGHTLY!

SAFETY

Everyone in the vehicle should always have a seat belt and use it.

DO NOT ALLOW ANYONE TO STAND WHILE THE VEHICLE IS MOVING. Standing in the vehicle and holding onto the roll bar can be very dangerous. If the vehicle hits a rock or log, it can catapult a person completely out of the vehicle.

Stay clear of tow straps and cables when winching.

Soft top vehicles should have a roll bar.

Be sure your vehicle and tires are in good condition.

Tell someone where you are going and when you expect to be back.

Travel with at least one other vehicle.

Carry at least minimal survival gear at all times.

Know your limits and the vehicle's limits – every vehicle will react differently in rough conditions.

Do not show off!

Alcohol and driving are not compatible.

KEEP YOUR ARMS AND LEGS INSIDE OF THE VEHICLE AT ALL TIMES.

Never throw cigarette butts out the vehicle because of potential fire danger.

When going off-road in dry conditions, be careful of starting a fire in dry grass from the intense heat of your vehicle's catalytic converter.

HOW TO PREPARE YOUR VEHICLE FOR ROUGH, OFF-HIGHWAY TRAILS

TOW HOOKS - All vehicles should have tow hooks on the front and the rear. They should be rated at a minimum of 20,000#, and should be properly mounted to the frame (NEVER on body panels, bumpers or suspension parts) with high strength bolts and reinforcing backing plates. Never weld hooks in place, as the heat may crystallize the metal which may cause failure of either the hook or of the part to which it is attached. A tow hook breaking off at the end of a tow strap has as much momentum as a cannonball, and has been known to go completely through a pickup truck tailgate. Please refer to the manufacturer for installation guidelines on proper tow hook installation.

SKID PLATES - Skid plates should be bolt-mounted on all vehicles to protect the underbody components. All Jeep vehicles equipped with the factory off-road package have all of these items included and are an excellent choice for going off-road.

ROCK RAILS - For trails rated 4 or higher, on a 1 - 10 scale, 10 being the most difficult, we recommend Rock Rails. We do not recommend Nerf Bars as they decrease the clearance of the vehicle. Rock Rails are designed to protect the rocker panels from rocks, stumps or logs. For more information, please see page 79 - 80.

HOW TO PREPARE YOUR VEHICLE FOR ROUGH, OFF-HIGHWAY TRAILS (continued)

ANTI-SWAY BAR DISCONNECT - Jeep Wrangler (YJ) owners should consider disconnecting the anti-sway bar when going on difficult trails. This allows more front-axle flexibility for better traction, but **BE SURE TO RECONNECT IT** when going back on the highway as this modification will affect steering stability. A reputable 4WD accessory shop will have the disconnect pin for your anti-sway bar. It is not necessary to disconnect the anti-sway bar on the Jeep Wrangler TJ.

TIRES - Larger tires should be a consideration. It is possible to upgrade to a 30 x 9.50 R15 or 31 x 10.50 R15 on Grand Cherokees, Cherokees and Wranglers. This will provide a little more ground clearance. We use stock Jeeps on the Rubicon Trail equipped with Goodyear MT/R 31" tires with a "C" load range. The new Goodyear MT/R is an excellent choice. The "C" load range gives you stronger sidewalls and could prevent a blowout or flat. The OE size on the 2003 Jeep Rubicon is LT245/75R16, a Goodyear Wrangler MT/R in load range "E". Many newer Jeep Cherokee models come with 16" tires - P225/75R16, P245/70R16, P235/65R17 and P235/70R16. Upgrades to load ranges of C, D, or E are possible. The load and cold inflation pressure imposed on the rim and wheel must not exceed the rim and wheel manufacturer's recommendation even though the tire may be approved for a higher load and maximum cold inflation pressure.

LIFT KITS - *Lift kits are not necessary;* however, a 1" - 2" lift on the Wrangler has worked out satisfactorily for extremely rough trails such as the Rubicon Trail.

BATTERY - Your battery should be securely mounted. An unsecured battery could fall over damaging your battery or engine.

THUMBS UP!

If you don't have power steering, drive with your thumbs up and out of the steering wheel.

If your tire hits a large rock or log, it will cause the steering wheel to spin out of your hands. If your thumbs are down, the steering wheel spokes can injure and even break them.

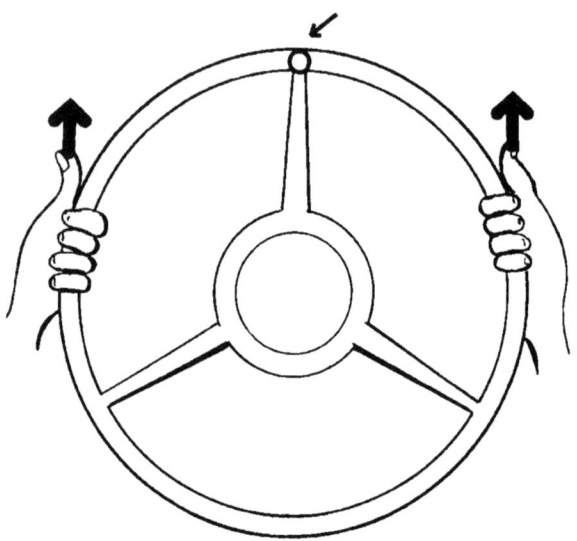

Helpful hint: Often in off-highway situations, the driver is not aware of the direction their tires are pointed. This can be corrected by placing a white dot or piece of tape on top of the steering wheel when the wheels are pointed straight ahead.

LOOK IN ALL DIRECTIONS

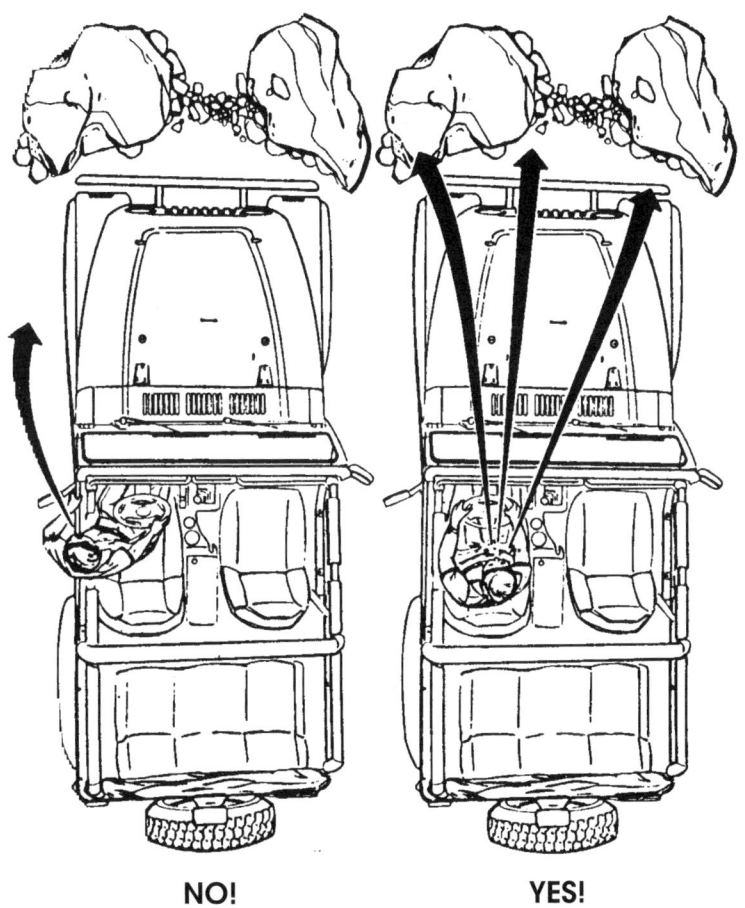

NO! **YES!**

Look over your hood and memorize what is ahead of you on the trail. Proceed slowly to crawl over obstacles.

If you put your head out of your vehicle and are watching your left front tire, there is a good chance you will get the right front tire in trouble.

OFF-ROAD DRIVING TECHNIQUES IN ROUGH TERRAIN

Automatic Transmission
Use low gear and low range. I suggest the two-footed driving method – left foot on the brake and right foot on the throttle. Feather both lightly to control your speed. If the vehicle slows down you may have to apply a little more throttle. If it speeds up you may have to apply a little brake. Speed and power are not the answer! GO SLOW - the slower the better.

Manual Transmission (Driving Without The Clutch)
Use low gear and low range. If your vehicle has locking hubs, be sure they are engaged. Start the vehicle in gear WITHOUT THE CLUTCH. KEEP BOTH FEET ON THE FLOOR. To start: Turn the key. Do not use the clutch and apply only slight throttle as needed. Drive slowly and crawl over the rocks and rough terrain. Idle over rough spots – slight throttle only as needed. KEEP YOUR FOOT OFF OF THE CLUTCH. If you start to slip or spin, apply a little more throttle and TURN THE STEERING WHEEL 1/2 TURN BACK AND FORTH. This will often provide a new grip. The important thing is to keep the vehicle moving. Keep your foot off of the clutch. Crawl over obstacles: THE SLOWER THE BETTER. Do not spin your wheels. To stop, just turn the key off – NO CLUTCH OR BRAKE IS NECESSARY. If the engine stalls going over a rough spot, do not use the clutch or brake. Simply turn the key again and apply very slight throttle if needed.

NOTE
A Jeep vehicle can be started this way with a one-foot high obstacle (like a stairway) right against the front wheels. In low gear ratios you can start the vehicle this way going uphill at up to a 45 degree angle. Using this method you have total vehicle control and will not burn up your clutch or harm the starter. EXCEPTION: There is an exception to the above technique; if the vehicle is in a very tight bind or up against a large rock or obstacle, and cannot move forward through use of the starter, then use the clutch to avoid burning up the starter.

HILLS

Hills cause many four-wheelers serious problems. If the hill is very steep and you don't feel confident that you or your vehicle can make it up, DO NOT ATTEMPT IT! When going up or down a hill, always try to go straight up or down. NEVER drive a hill at an angle as this could cause the vehicle to roll over.

Most vehicles will climb small, steep inclines, but not long steep hills. Speed and power are not necessarily the answer.

KEEP YOUR WHEELS ON THE GROUND AT ALL TIMES. One of the biggest misconceptions in four-wheeling today is caused by advertisements that show the vehicles flying through the air. This is NOT the proper or safe way to drive. Most of the vehicles used in making these advertisements are hauled to the junkyard after filming.

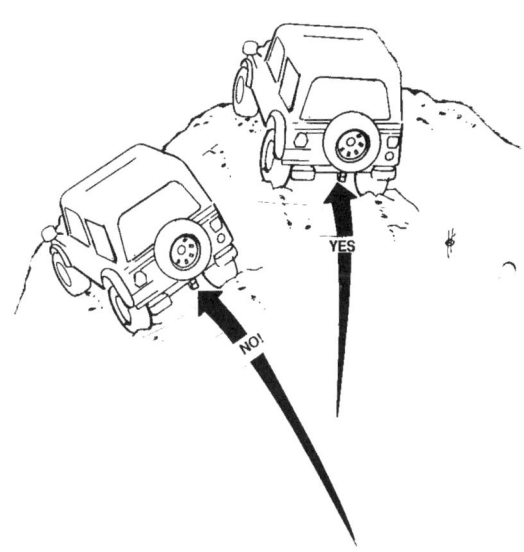

IF A HILL IS TOO STEEP, DO NOT ATTEMPT IT!

AVOID DRIVING SIDE HILL

If at all possible, avoid driving side hill. If you must, KNOW YOUR VEHICLE'S LIMITATIONS AND CENTER OF GRAVITY.

GOING UP A STEEP HILL

Remember there are many things that will affect going up a hill.

Tires and the type of tread: An all terrain tire with good tread will offer you the best traction.

Soil conditions: Damp soil gives you the best traction. Loose, dry soil or sand may cause a spin out. Wet or muddy soil can be the most difficult and dangerous and may cause you to lose control.

Know your limitations and the vehicle's limitations.

Be sure you know what is on the other side of a hill before going up and over. It is often a good idea to scout the hill's crest on foot before attempting to drive over it.

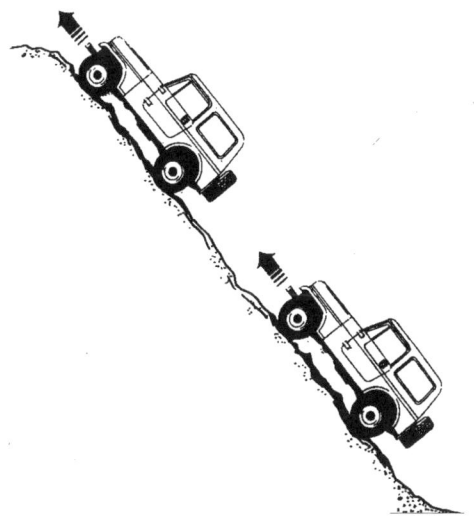

Apply more power as you start up a hill. If the front end of your vehicle begins to "chatter" (front end jumping up and down) back off the throttle slightly to keep all four wheels on the ground. If not, you may cause vehicle damage.

Ease up on power as you approach the top.

If you stall, put your vehicle into reverse and back <u>straight down</u> the hill. Avoid turning as you could lose control and possibly cause the vehicle to roll over.

GOING DOWN A STEEP HILL

DO NOT USE YOUR CLUTCH WHEN GOING DOWN A STEEP OR ROCKY HILL!

Always use the vehicle's compression. In a vehicle with a manual transmission, use the lowest gears and compression. Do not ride your clutch. Pump the brakes lightly if necessary. In an automatic, use low range and the lowest drive setting.

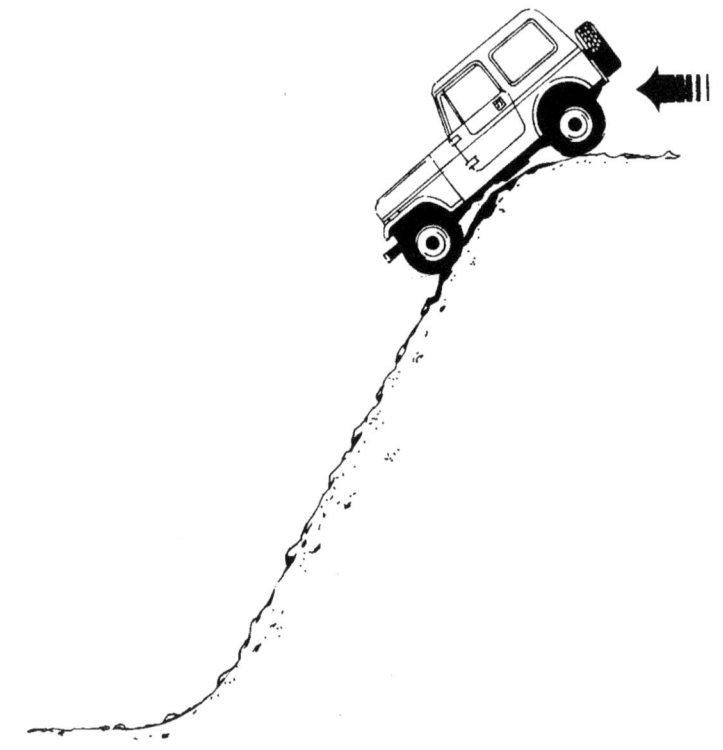

With automatic transmissions, feather your brakes lightly. If you start to slide, turn in the direction of the slide as on snow or ice. If you have ABS (anti-lock braking system), do not pump the brakes.

KNOW YOUR ANGLE OF APPROACH AND DEPARTURE

When crossing a ditch, know your angle of approach and departure.

Vehicle length and type will affect angle of approach and departure.

DON'T HIGH CENTER

When going over large rocks, a hill or a mound of dirt, be careful not to high center.

If you get high centered, try putting rocks or anything else available under the tires and then gently rock the vehicle while turning the wheels back and forth. In some conditions, you may require a jack to free yourself.

LOSING TRACTION

If you start to lose traction in sand, mud or snow, turn your steering wheel back and forth slowly. This will generally allow the tires to get a fresh grip and pull you through.

If you lose complete traction, **STOP!** Do not spin your wheels, as this will usually dig you in deeper.

Remember, speed and power are not the answer. Keep forward momentum at a steady pace.

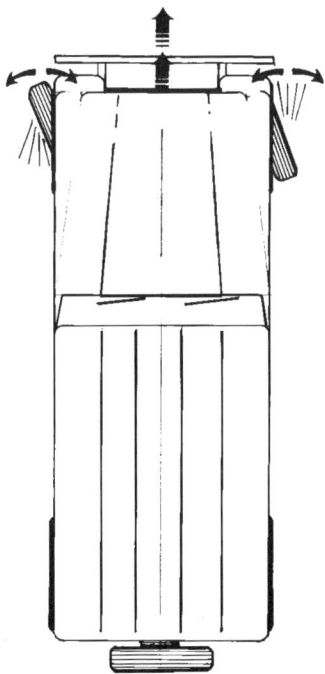

If your tires start to spin, a slight brake application with your left foot while maintaining throttle pressure, will stop wheel spin and maintain forward momentum.

ROCKS

Do not straddle rocks. A vehicle with 6" of ground clearance will not go over an 8" rock.

NO!

If you hear rocks or other obstacles scraping against your vehicles rock rails or skid plates, don't panic. These accessories are doing their job protecting your vehicle.

YES!

Ideal speed for rock crawling is one to three miles per hour.

Be careful not to high center! **YES!**

ROCKS (continued)

Rubicon Trail, California

Proper driving techniques.
Put your tires on top of the rocks as these photos demonstrate.
Do not straddle large rocks.

Rubicon Trail, California

SAND

Sand can vary in different parts of the country. In Florida, you can drive for 300 miles in hard sand and not have any problems. In the desert in Southern California, you would have to deflate your tires to 20 lbs. +/-.

Generally the additional speed and power offered by 4WD high are appropriate for driving in sand. Sometimes, however, low range and drive will work more efficiently in sand and will provide more torque in certain situations. You may need to experiment with both high and low range depending on the surface conditions of the sand you are driving on.

If you get stuck, dig out around the wheels. Use your floor mats under the wheels for traction. If water is available, wet the sand in front of the wheels - this will provide a firmer base. If necessary, air down to 8 or 10 pounds. Rock back and forth and sideways, and once moving forward just keep a good steady forward motion - don't spin your wheels, as you will only make it worse. Use your hub cabs as a shovel if needed.

When driving in sand dunes, be sure your vehicle has a flag on the radio antenna or a mast. This allows four-wheelers on the other side of a dune to know where you are.

Note: Whenever going off-road, be sure that you know where you are going and don't travel by yourself. Tell someone where you are going and when you expect to be back.

Sand Mountain, Nevada

SNOW AND ICE

Always use caution when driving in snow and on ice. Make sure that you have good mud and snow or All Terrain (AT) tires. When you have to slow down or stop, pump your brakes lightly. Do not slam on your brakes, as this may cause you to skid. If you start to slide, turn **into** the direction of the slide and brake lightly. If you get stuck in snow or mud, do not race the motor and spin the wheels as you will probably dig a deeper hole. Never travel over 25 miles per hour in snow or ice conditions. Be very cautious of black ice.* **If you have ABS brakes, apply gentle pressure. Do not pump!**

When moving through snow or over obstacles, if you have any forward motion at all (regardless of how slow it is), keep the vehicle moving. If you start to get stuck, turn your wheels back and forth. This will transfer power to the wheels where you need the traction. Make sure to keep your forward momentum. If you do get stuck, stop and analyze your situation. If you have to put chains on your 4WD vehicle, chain the front wheels.

If you get stuck, dig out around the tires and place your floor mats in front of the tires. Gently rock the vehicle back and forth and turn the steering wheel from side to side until you have traction. Decrease tire pressures to 10 to 20 pounds if necessary for greater traction.

* Black Ice - This occurs when rain or melting snow freezes and forms a thin invisible layer of ice over the pavement creating a dangerous icy condition.

DUST

When driving on dusty roads, roll up your windows and turn on the air conditioner or fan. This will help pressurize the cab and help keep the dust out. Be sure the fresh air vent is closed.

MEADOWS

Only drive through meadows on established roads or trails. Respect and do not abuse public or private lands.

MUD

Before entering a mud hole, analyze the situation. How deep is it? How long is it? Are there any hidden obstacles? Always keep forward momentum even if you are only crawling. Turning the wheels back and forth often gives the tires a new grip. If you do get stuck, try backing up and then going forward again. If you can't go forward, back up and find another way around.

Use a stick to check the depth of a mud hole. If there aren't any tire tracks going out the other side, think again before going into it.

Unless you are moving forward, don't spin your tires. They will just dig deeper. If you get stuck, dig out around your tires then place rocks, logs or other firm material underneath for traction.

Important: Check differentials, transmission, transfer case and brakes after crossing deep mud or water. Mud may also pack in the wheel after driving in deep sticky mud. This may cause vibrations on the highway. Use a pressure hose to wash the mud out of the wheels.

RUTS

If you are in a deep rut in mud or snow and can't get out, dig two small trenches at a 45 degree angle, either right or left, and place the materials removed into the rut.

Drive forward slowly and the vehicle should drive up and out of the rut.

If the ruts are too deep to drive in, move to the left or right and drive parallel to the existing ruts.

RUTS (continued)

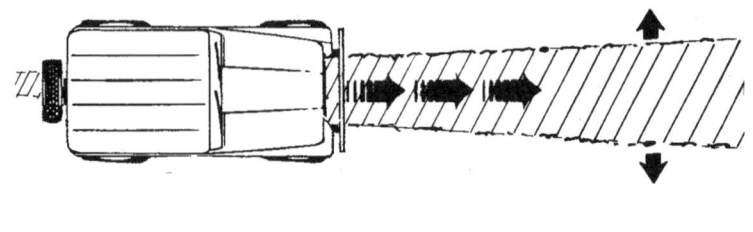

If you find yourself in a situation where you must traverse a rut....

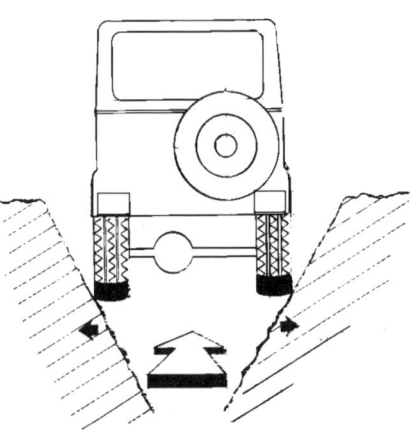

Go slow and straddle the rut when possible. If the rut becomes too wide, ease into it keeping your vehicle level and ride on the tire edge or even the sidewall of the tire.

Judge the trail over your hood or have your passenger outside of the vehicle guide you. Remember to try to keep centered in the rut and keep the vehicle as level as possible.

RUTS (continued)

Keep your vehicle level while driving ruts

CROSSING STREAMS

Be extremely cautious of fast moving water, and remember that even clear water can be very deceiving. Be extra cautious of muddy water.

If you can't see the bottom and you don't know how deep it is, you or your passenger should cross the stream by foot first, or use a stick to check the depth before crossing it in your vehicle. Once again, be cautious of fast moving water.

Before attempting to go into water above your vehicle's axles, check for the location of your air intake. Some vehicles have these intakes located by the bumper. Crossing water in a vehicle so equipped may result in severe damage from water being drawn into the engine.

If the water level is up to your headlights, take your seat belts off and open the windows for an easy escape if necessary.

If you are going to cross deep water, do not let your spark plugs or distributor get wet. Go slow. Place a jacket or a piece of canvas or cardboard in front of the radiator to deflect water.

If your engine stalls in deep water, DO NOT try to restart it, as you may cause serious damage to your vehicle.

When crossing, go slow. Do not make a wave in front of the vehicle.

Cross streams in designated areas only - avoid breaking down banks when entering or leaving a stream.

CROSSING STREAMS (continued)

Start downstream from where you would like to cross. Drive at a slight angle UP into the current. If there is a strong current, it will move the vehicle downstream. This will take you to your desired point of exit.

While crossing steams, watch for large submerged rocks or obstacles.

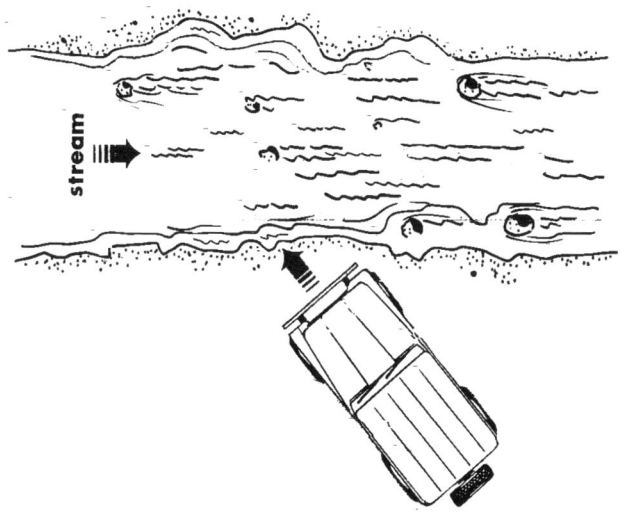

AFTER BEING IN MUD OR DEEP WATER, IT IS A GOOD IDEA TO CHECK YOUR DIFFERENTIALS AND TRANSFER CASE FOR WATER OR MUD. AFTER DRIVING IN WATER, TEST YOUR BRAKES. WET BRAKES FEEL AND WORK LIKE NO BRAKES. IN ORDER TO DRY YOUR BRAKES, SIMPLY RIDE THE BRAKE PEDAL LIGHTLY WHILE THE VEHICLE IS MOVING.

CROSSING STREAMS (continued)

When crossing, go slow. Do not make a wave in front of the vehicle.

This Jeep may be moving a little too quickly.

WATER DEPTH

Up to axles – Generally OK

Bumper depth – Use caution, check air intake

Bottom of headlights – Use caution

Headlights – Avoid if at all possible (remember, seat belts off, windows open. This will make for an easy escape from the vehicle in an emergency.)

Headlights
Bumper
Axles

If you stall, do not attempt to start or run the engine in deep water or where water can enter the air intake.

CROSS STREAMS ONLY IN APPROVED AND DESIGNATED AREAS!

CROSSING A LOG OR TREE

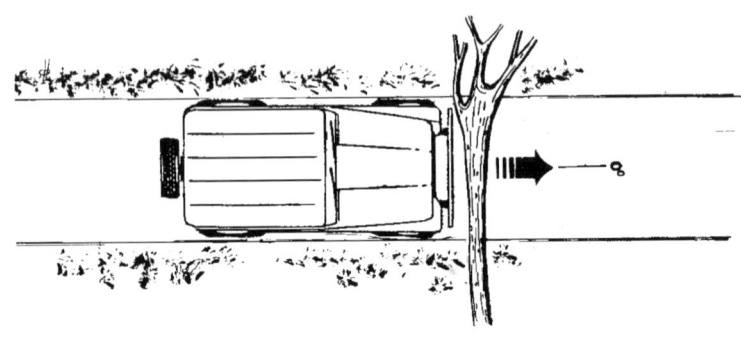

When you encounter a log or tree across the trail, it may be easier to cross at a slight angle rather than straight on. Be sure of your ground clearance. If you only have 8" of clearance, you will not be able to cross over a 12" log. In this case, you could build a ramp on both sides of the log with small logs, rocks or dirt.

THREE POINT TURN FOR TURNING AROUND ON A NARROW ROAD

Step 1: Use low range and 1st gear. Pull up to the edge of the road and put the vehicle into reverse and back up the hill.

Step 2: Use power as needed to go up the bank high enough to turn the front wheels hard in the direction you want to go.

Step 3: Drive back onto the road in the opposite direction.

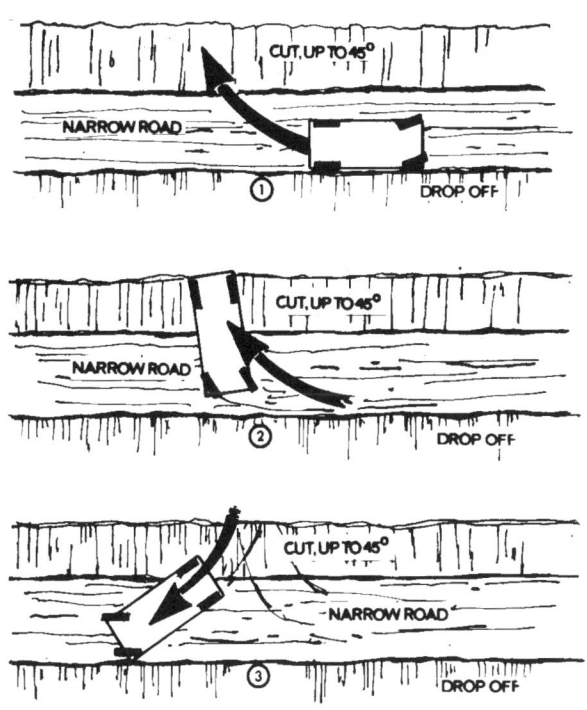

THREE POINT TURN FOR TURNING AROUND ON A NARROW ROAD (continued)

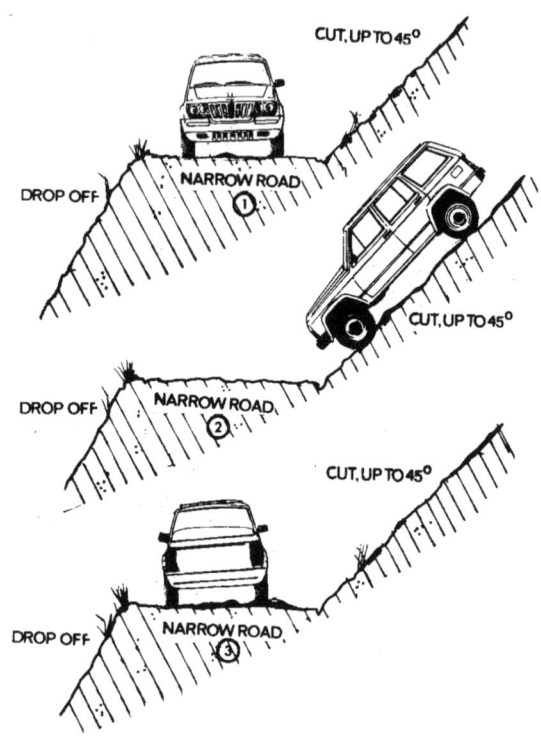

Use extreme caution with this maneuver.

ROUGH COUNTRY DRIVING SUMMARY

Use low range – 4-wheel drive and lowest gear.

If you have a manual transmission, start the vehicle in gear without the clutch (see page 12), pressing the throttle a little as needed.

If you have an automatic transmission, remember to SHIFT INTO NEUTRAL TO SHIFT TO LOW RANGE. Use low range and your lowest drive gear. Use the left foot on the brake and right foot on the throttle. Apply throttle only as needed.

Keep your foot off the clutch at all times. Start and stop with your key. Always use compression going downhill. Idle over obstacles. It might be necessary to use the throttle slightly going uphill.

Don't straddle large rocks. Put your tire on top of the rocks and crawl over them slowly. Use throttle only as needed.

Maintain adequate speed. Going too fast off-road can damage your vehicle. Drive slowly. If you start to spin or slip, give a little throttle and turn the steering wheel slowly 1/2 turn back and forth.

Keep moving once you are committed. Proper momentum and smooth handling are the key.

TIRES

A good radial AT (all-terrain) or radial MS (mud and snow) tire is sufficient for most off-highway driving circumstances. Radial tires are ideal since they provide a larger footprint than other tires of the same size. This larger area of contact will provide more traction on rough terrain.

I recommend a tire with a "C" or "D" load range. These load ranges indicate a stronger sidewall construction, which are recommended for driving in rough terrain.

TIRE PRESSURE

For on-highway conditions, always follow the manufacturer's recommended tire pressures. When you venture off-road, however, you may want to lower the tire pressure. Letting some air out of the tires makes them softer and expands the tire footprint for greater flotation, resulting in more traction when driving over rocks or in sand. Lower tire pressure will also cushion the vehicle's ride.

Different conditions may require different tire pressures depending on your vehicle. Ideal air down situations for rough, off-road travel:

Trail Condition	Ideal Pressure	Extreme Air Down For Emergency Conditions Only
Rocky terrain (Rubicon)	22 to 26 lbs	22 to 26 lbs
Loose desert sand	22 to 26 lbs	8 to 10 lbs
Deep mud	22 to 24 lbs	10 to 12 lbs
Deep snow	26 to 28 lbs	8 to 10 lbs

But remember that too little tire pressure, especially with stock tires, can result in the tire being pushed off of the rim, causing it to go flat.

As soon as you get back on surfaced roads, return your tires to normal air pressures. Don't guess; carry a good quality pressure gauge with you. Under-inflated tires can influence vehicle handling, traction and tread wear. Correct air inflation is vital to a tire's long service life.

TIRE PRESSURE (continued)

Directional tires offer a more aggressive tread and are usually used in heavy mud and snow areas. For general use, the radial AT (all terrain) tire does an excellent job.

Tires on all four wheels should always be of the same size and type. To help even out the wear, tires should be rotated on a regular basis.

Tires should be inspected periodically for cuts, bulges or any other signs of damage. Repairs should be made only by authorized tire centers.

Flat Tire Tip – Your tire has been pushed away from the rim and has gone flat, you may be able to reinflate the tire. Jack the wheel up, and if an air source is available, use it to reinflate the tire. Generally, this will reseat the tire on the wheel. A can of air and repair (available at automotive parts stores) is a handy item.

Be careful of sharp rocks or limbs that could puncture the side walls.

Carry a full-size spare tire and wheel.

REMEMBER TO REINFLATE YOUR TIRES WHEN YOU ARE BACK ON SOLID GROUND!

TIRE RECOMMENDATIONS

In 1978, a group of Jeep enthusiasts and I, with five CJ-7's, completed a record-breaking trip beginning at the southern tip of South America (Tierra del Fuego, Chile) and ending in Prudhoe Bay, Alaska. Our five Jeeps were equipped with Goodyear RT tires (31 x 11.50 x 15). I put 21,000 miles on my Jeep and did not experience a flat tire throughout the entire trip.

I highly recommend the new Goodyear Wrangler MT/R. It is a great multi-purpose tire with three-ply sidewalls and a tread to match any terrain. It has been tested and proven on the Rubicon Trail.

GOODYEAR TIRES

A. WRANGLER MT/R - Goodyear's latest and greatest off-road tire is aggressive enough to tame the Rubicon Trail. Some have said the R in the tire name stands for Rubicon, because that was where the tire was introduced and showcased. It actually stands for Maximum Traction /Reinforced. This Goodyear muscle tire was designed for 4WD vehicles that work on the rocks, but its aggressive stance on the highway will make it popular for the everyday driver. The tire's construction - three high modulus polyester plies in the sidewall and  a high-tech silica/carbon black compound - makes the Wrangler MT/R's sidewall puncture-resistant. A working tread that extends down the sidewalls provides added traction off road.

B. WRANGLER AT/S - The first dual traction lug channel tire for pickup trucks and SUVs offers excellent treadwear and off-road traction as well as a quiet ride on highways. These channels are designed to prevent mud and snow from sticking in the tread grooves. The centerline between the channels provides solidity for improved noise characteristics. Countless blades and notches offer improved wet, snow and off-road performance.

GOODYEAR TIRES (continued)

C. WRANGLER GS-A - This asymmetric tire provides more tread on the outside shoulder for greater cornering power. Hefty tread lugs and a squared-off inside shoulder delivers improved traction in the rain and snow. Deep, wide groves in the center offer improved handling on wet roads. Reinforced sidewalls and rugged tread compounds provide long tire life.

D. WORKHORSE EXTRA GRIP RADIAL - An aggressive tread pattern was designed to provide greater grip on loose gravel and the back roads of farms and industrial work sites. The Workhorse Extra Grip offers added traction in commercial applications, such as logging, forestry, mining, construction and gas/oil drilling operations. A deep, channeled tread pattern and aggressive shoulder notches supply increased traction when it's needed most. In the winter, studs can be installed for improved snow and ice traction.

WINCHING

IF YOU ARE STUCK, before you pull out your winch line, analyze the situation and determine what has immobilized your vehicle.

Decide whether to continue forward or go back. If you are severely "hung up" on a rock or stump, you should consider jacking the vehicle up and putting something under the tires to clear the obstacle.

Use a direct one-line pull to a tree or large rock. If you are really stuck, use the pulley or "snatch block" and double back to the vehicle. Use your tree strap and clevis pin mounted low at the base of the tree. DO NOT WRAP YOUR WINCH LINE AROUND THE TREE AS IT COULD KILL THE TREE.

If necessary, you can winch at an angle. Be cautious of cable buildup on one side of the winch drum. Do not try to guide the cable while winching as this could result in serious injury. After you are clear of the obstacle, pull the cable out and rewind.

WHENEVER POSSIBLE, USE THE POWER OF YOUR VEHICLE WITH THE POWER OF THE WINCH. YOUR CONTROL CABLE IS LONG ENOUGH TO REACH INTO THE DRIVER'S WINDOW OF THE VEHICLE. MAKE SURE YOU ARE USING THE VEHICLE'S POWER AND THE WINCH'S POWER GENTLY AND SMOOTHLY – NO JERKING. DON'T DRIVE OVER THE WINCH CABLE.

If you have two vehicles and one winch:
1. Connect the winch hook to the vehicle that is stuck.
2. Put the vehicle that is stuck into its lowest gear range and gently apply power to assist the winch.
3. Set the brake on the anchor vehicle to hold it in place or, if necessary, place a rock or log in front of wheels.
4. The anchor vehicle could also be put into reverse to gently pull the stuck vehicle. Using this technique you have the power of two vehicles and the winch.

If you have two vehicles and both are equipped with winches, you can use the power of both winches.

BASIC, SIMPLE WINCHING

Direct pull with the winch engaged. Both vehicles should be in 4WD low range. Put winching vehicle into reverse gear and slowly apply power while winching. The stuck vehicle should be in first gear and gently applying power while being winched.

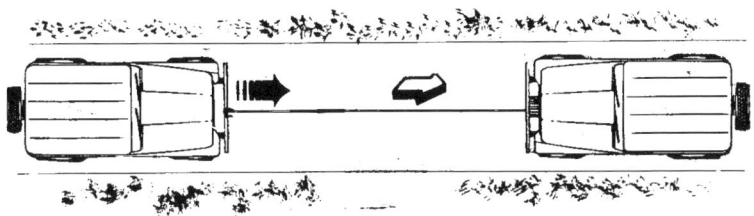

When hooking to a vehicle, hook to a properly mounted tow hook or the frame. **Do not hook to the bumper!**

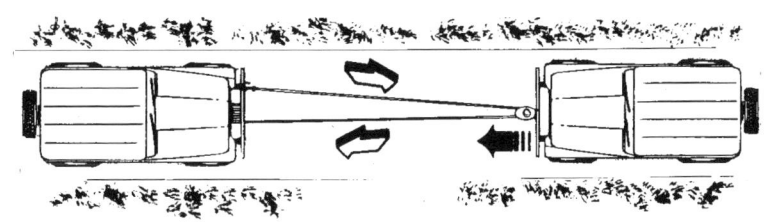

Double blocking using a snatch block or pulley effectively doubles the capacity of your winch. Use this technique for more difficult situations.

WINCHING ACCESSORIES

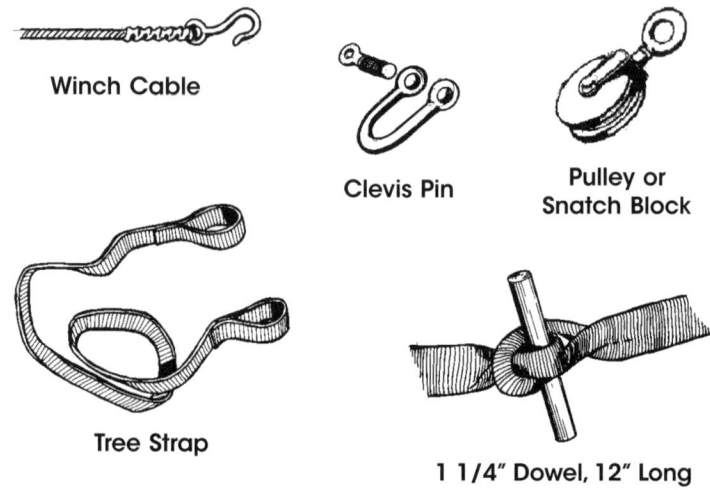

Winch Cable

Clevis Pin

Pulley or Snatch Block

Tree Strap

1 1/4" Dowel, 12" Long

I strongly recommend the **Ramsey Winch Accessory Kit** which contains a snatch block, steel shackle, tree strap and gloves.

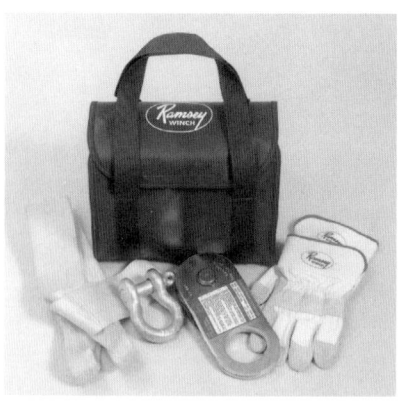

USING YOUR WINCH

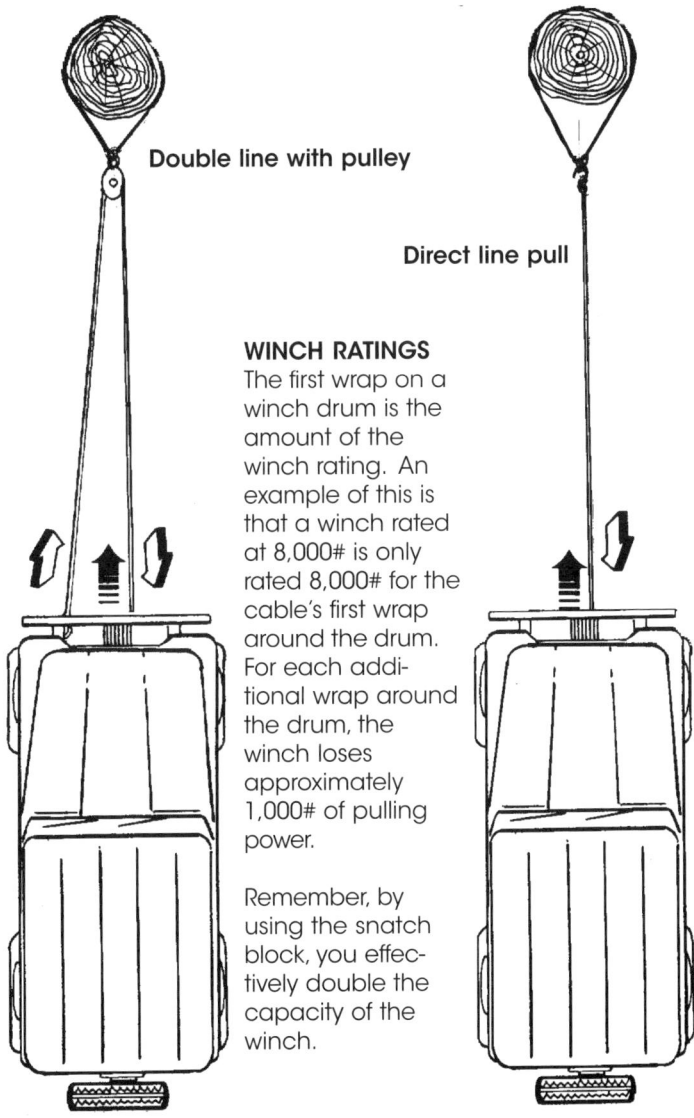

Double line with pulley

Direct line pull

WINCH RATINGS

The first wrap on a winch drum is the amount of the winch rating. An example of this is that a winch rated at 8,000# is only rated 8,000# for the cable's first wrap around the drum. For each additional wrap around the drum, the winch loses approximately 1,000# of pulling power.

Remember, by using the snatch block, you effectively double the capacity of the winch.

USING YOUR WINCH (continued)

Direct line pull

LARGE TREE ACROSS ROAD

Example:
Put tow strap around rock or tree as shown with pulley. Winch tree back until you can pass.

GETTING BACK ON THE ROAD

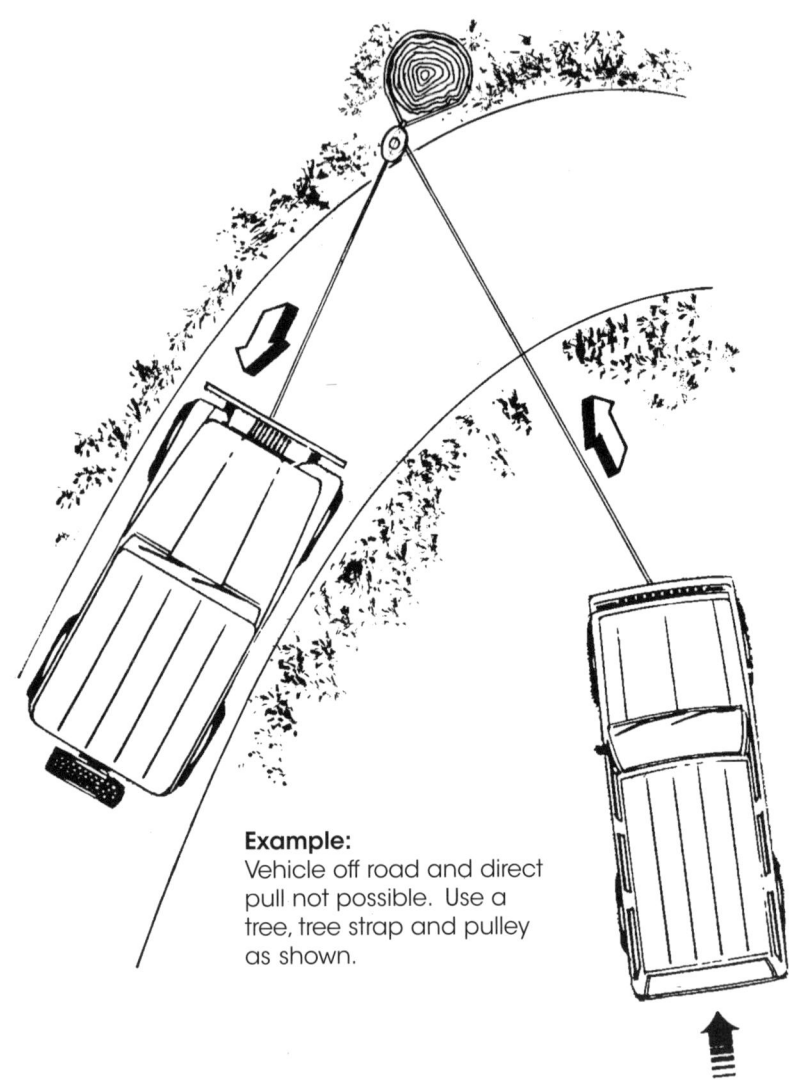

Example:
Vehicle off road and direct pull not possible. Use a tree, tree strap and pulley as shown.

ALWAYS USE A TREE STRAP AND PLACE LOW ON THE TREE

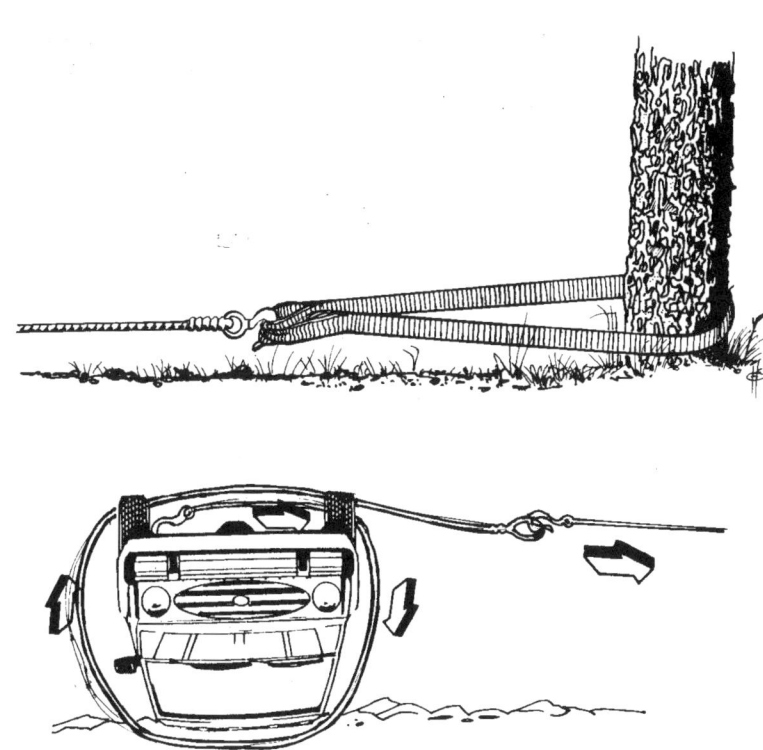

If a vehicle rolls and you are attempting to right it with a winch, don't hook onto the high side of the frame and attempt to pull it upright. Wrap a tow strap or even the cable itself all the way around the vehicle as shown. This effectively multiplies the torque of the winch and gives more positive control over the operation. When working with a bare winch line, be careful that it isn't laid unprotected over sharp objects on the vehicle's undercarriage or body.

SNATCHUM STRAP

A 20' nylon rope or strap with 20,000# or more breaking test strength is used to get a stuck vehicle free in mud or sand. I personally recommend using only straps with at least a 20,000# breaking test strength, and only straps constructed without hooks (loops only) and from non-stretch nylon strap.

The pulling vehicle will back up with slack (2' - 3') then pull forward with the stuck vehicle applying power. The nylon strap tightens and pulls the vehicle free. A 1 1/4" hardwood dowel (12" long) works great for connecting two tow straps. You can also slip the loop end of a tow strap through the spring shackle and use the 1 1/4" dowel or a piece of wood to hold it (see photo on page 50).

Never connect two straps with a clevis pin.

Never use tow straps with metal hooks.

Generally, a stuck vehicle can be freed with only a slight tug by the pulling vehicle.

SNATCHUM STRAP (continued)

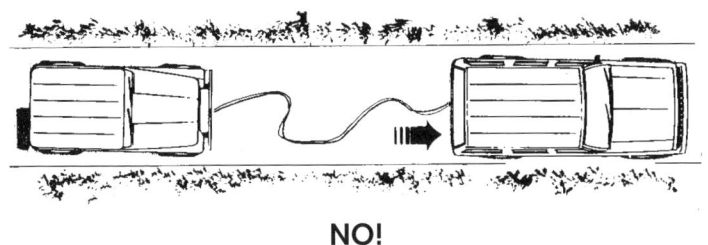

NO!

Caution: Be extremely careful of tow straps, ropes and winch cables. They have been known to break and become VERY dangerous projectiles. Be sure everyone is at a safe distance of at least 30' or more away whenever there is a strapping / winching situation.

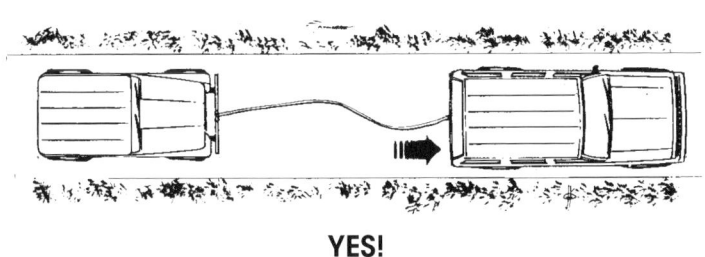

YES!

A SHORT, EASY PULL WILL GENERALLY FREE A STUCK VEHICLE.

PROPER WAY TO CONNECT TWO STRAPS TOGETHER

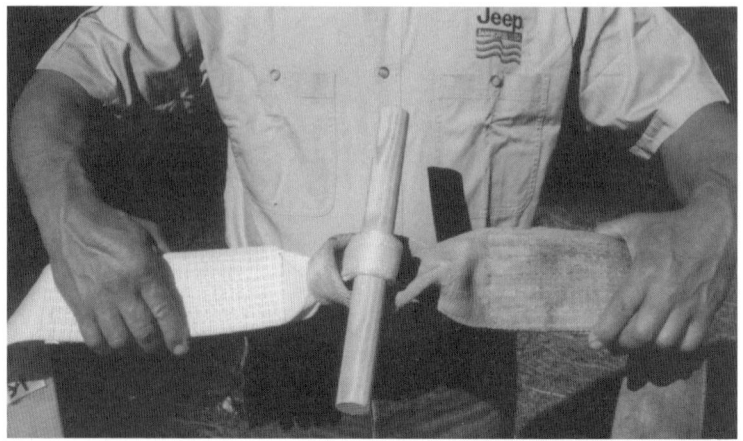

A safe way to connect two tow straps together: Use a 1 1/4" hardwood dowel (12" long) works great for connecting two tow straps. A strong limb will also work. You can also slip the loop end of a tow strap through the spring shackle and use the 1 1/4" dowel or a piece of wood to hold it. Never use a clevis pin. If a strap breaks it may become a deadly projectile (see page 51).

WHY WE DON'T USE TOW STRAPS WITH HOOKS OR CONNECT THEM TOGETHER WITH A CLEVIS PIN

The clevis pin is beneath the left front tire. It went through the back of the vehicle, the seat and the windshield, narrowly missing the driver. **Never use a tow strap with a hook or connect two tow straps with a clevis pin.**

WINCHING SUMMARY

ALWAYS use gloves when winching. Cables often develop burrs and can cause injuries.

ALWAYS place a jacket, large piece of canvas, towel or anything you have over the winch cable while winching. This will act as a parachute in the event of a cable breaking.

NEVER stand by or straddle a winch cable when the winch is being used.

ONLY hook to the frame or spring shackle if tow hooks are not available. Use caution when you hook onto a vehicle to avoid a potentially dangerous situation or damage to the vehicle.

NEVER jerk with the winch line or use like a tow strap.

DON'T pull your hook into the roller on the winch. Release power approximately three feet from the winch and spool in gently.

DON'T try to get the winch to spool evenly while winching. You can always pull the cable out after you are done and rewind it neatly.

DON'T drive over your winch cable.

DON'T wrap your winch cable around something that will kink it.

DON'T hook onto your winch cable. Hooking to your cable will cut and weaken the cable.

NEVER use your winch to support or lift a person.

ALWAYS make sure there are at least **five wraps of cable** remaining on the drum before winching.

ALWAYS keep everyone as far away as possible from cable when winching; at least a minimum of 30' or more.

WINCHING SUMMARY (continued)

Use extreme caution when reeling the cable in. Keep your hands and fingers clear.

When you are finished winching and begin to reel in the cable, leave approximately three feet of cable and the winch hook free to connect to the tow hook or bumper.

Remember to disengage the winch and disconnect the control cable when you are done.

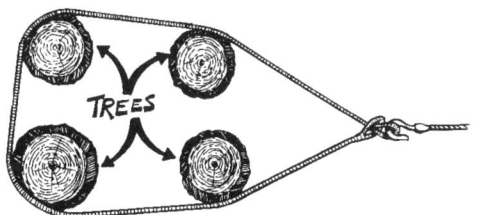

If you do not have a large tree to winch to, loop your tree strap or tow strap low around small trees or heavy brush.

NEVER WRAP YOUR CABLE AROUND A TREE OR HOOK ONTO YOUR WINCH CABLE. Hooking to your cable will cut and weaken the cable. Wrapping your cable around a tree will damage or possibly kill the tree. This is illegal in many states and could lead to a large fine.

WHAT WINCH DO I PERSONALLY RECOMMEND?

RAMSEY WINCH

Why do I prefer Ramsey Winches?

My many years of personal experience using Ramsey winches include the crossing of the Darien Gap. This was a trip through the jungles of Panama and Columbia. Our five Jeep CJ7's were equipped with Ramsey 8,000# winches. They were used two or three times daily under extreme conditions and performed flawlessly. With their low amperage draw, we did not have any problems with battery drainage. One day we went 500 feet in nine hours, winching up hills as high as 160 feet at angles up to 85 degrees. We named this area Ramsey Ravine. Without our Ramsey winches, the expedition's success would not have been possible (see page 69 for more information on the Expedicion de las Americas).

What size winch do you need?

Small vehicle: 6,000 # or 8,000#

Mid to full-size: 8,000 # or 9,000 #

For heavy-duty work and off-highway use: the worm drive family of winches, the RE 8,000, RE 10,000 or 12,0000, PROPLUS8000, 9,000, or 9,500 or the new Platinum 9500.

WHAT TO TAKE FOR OFF-HIGHWAY TRIPS

- CB radio and/or cellular phone
- Area maps
- GPS, if available
- A good first aid kit
- Shovel
- Axe or saw
- A good jack
- Basic tools - pliers, wrenches, screwdrivers, jumper cables
- Fire extinguisher
- Full-size spare tire
- Tire pressure gauge, tire pump, tire repair kit or small can of tire sealant & air pressure
- Radiator Stop Leak
- Tow rope / snatchum strap
- Gloves
- Baling wire and duct tape
- Extra motor oil, 1 or 2 quarts
- Extra gasoline, enough for round-trip
- Flashlight and extra batteries
- Plastic sheet or tarp, 6' x 6'
- Shelter (tent) & foul weather gear
- Sleeping bags
- Food & lots of water for the amount of time gone - can opener, paper towels and garbage bags
- Dehydrated foods which take little space and last a long time
- A good knife
- Matches, kept in a plastic bag so they don't get wet
- Toilet paper and zip locks for tissue disposal
- Winch owners: a winch kit, including a tree strap, a clevis pin, a snatch block or pulley, and a 1 1/4" dowel (12" long)

ROAD COURTESY

Courtesy is contagious –

If you are being overtaken by another vehicle, pull over and allow the other vehicle to pass.

Vehicles going uphill have the right-of-way. On steep inclines, loss of climbing momentum could mean a loss of traction or an engine stall and could cause a dangerous situation.

When you leave your vehicle, park completely off of the trail. Remember to Tread Lightly!

Four-wheeling takes skill and good common sense.

Alcohol and driving are NOT compatible at any time!

We recommend you join a four wheel drive club. To locate a club in your area, please contact:

United Four Wheel Drive Associations
4505 West 700
Shelbyville, IN 46176-9678
Phone: 800-44-UFWDA (800-448-3932)
Fax: 317-729-5862
E-mail: membership@ufwda.org
Web Site: www.ufwda.org

REPORT VIOLATIONS

Take license numbers of poachers or off-roaders who are tearing up the land or littering, and give license numbers to a ranger or law enforcement officer as soon as possible.

HELPFUL HINTS

If you have a broken radiator and no Stop Leak, pinch off the tubes that are leaking and put pepper in the radiator. If you don't have any pepper, try one or two raw eggs. If these don't work, you can use a handful or two of dry cow manure.

Freezing ice tea or water in one gallon plastic jugs keeps the contents of your ice chest cold. It will also provide a refreshing cold drink as it thaws.

Survival Tips
If you break down, be calm and stay with your vehicle. Use your CB radio or cellular phone to summon help. Remember to protect yourself from the elements. Avoid running your vehicle's battery down. If you are carrying at least basic survival gear, you should be able to hold out until help arrives. As mentioned earlier, **always** tell someone where you are going and when you expect to be back.

THE NEW "RUBICON" JEEP

PROPER USE OF YOUR TRU-LOC™ LOCKING DIFFERENTIALS:

With the lower 4:1 gearing, your Rubicon is capable of severe trails without the continuous use of the "lockers". Remember, the rear differential operates as a limited slip unit when the locker is disengaged.

Under very rough conditions, engage the rear locker and if extremely rough, engage the front locker to get over a particular rough spot. Disengage when over the toughest obstacles.

Do not operate with lockers engaged unless needed.

Keeping the front locker engaged will make steering much more difficult and adds unnecessary stress on the front drivetrain. On wet, muddy, uneven or steep trails, the lockers will give the extra traction you need.

With a manual transmission, you can start and stop without disengaging the clutch by temporarily bypassing the clutch interlock circuit. Refer to owner's manual for procedure.

OFF-HIGHWAY DRIVING TIPS SUMMARY

KNOW YOUR LIMITS AND THE VEHICLE'S LIMITS.

Everyone in the vehicle should wear seat belts at all times.

Don't allow anyone to stand in a moving vehicle.

Look over your hood, and continuously analyze and memorize the trail ahead of you while driving it.

Remember, slow and easy - speed and power are not required off-road.

Don't spin your wheels or apply too much power.

Always keep your wheels on the ground - avoid front end chatter.

If your wheels start to spin, slowly move the steering wheel back and forth 1/2 turn.

Always keep adequate forward momentum even if you are only crawling. Smooth, easy power is better than too much power.

Drive slow and in a safe, common sense manner.

Don't endanger yourself or your passengers.

Keep arms and legs in the vehicle.

Don't litter—carry a litter bag with you. Leave a clean trail and a good image of off-road enthusiasts. Enjoy the heritage and back country our nation has to offer. If you drive your vehicle slow and easy, you can enjoy the many miles of scenery that would normally not be seen by the general public.

OFF-HIGHWAY DRIVING TIPS SUMMARY (continued)

I have said many times that once you have mastered off-road driving you can drive holding a half cup of coffee or water and never spill a drop. Visualize having a crate of raw eggs in the back of your vehicle with your goal being not to break any. This is the way you want to drive in rough country.

Respect the rights and property of others. **Always** get permission before you enter private lands and leave gates as you find them.

THE JEEP JAMBOREE USA STORY

In 1953, Mark A. Smith and a group of Georgetown, California Rotarians organized the Jeepers Jamboree over the rugged Rubicon Trail as a method for promoting tourism in their remote Sierra Nevada foothills town. This was the modest beginning of Jeep Jamboree USA, a series of off-road adventures for Jeep owners, which has grown to span the country. Each year, over 7,500 Jeep enthusiasts learn about their own capabilities, as well as those of their Jeep vehicles, while exploring America's magnificent back country. From the wooded forests of Maine, to Utah's painted deserts, to the ultimate challenge offered by the mighty Rubicon Trail itself, Jeep Jamboree USA offers an unparalleled range of expertly guided off-road experiences to Jeep enthusiasts. The Jamboree season runs February through October featuring over 35 trips of varying difficulties, ranging from mild trail runs suitable for curious first-timers to obstacle-rich routes which challenge even veteran off-roaders. For more information, please contact:

Jeep Jamboree USA
P. O. Box 1601
Georgetown, CA 95634
PH: (530) 333-4777   FX: (530) 333-2844
E-mail: jeepjam@jeepjam.com
Web site: www.jeepjamboreeusa.com

PUBLIC LANDS ARE FOR ALL TO USE AND ENJOY!

THE JEEP JAMBOREE USA STORY (continued)

Typical terrain on a Jeep Jamboree.

Grand Cherokee crossing a log bridge on a Jeep Jamboree USA trail.

THE JEEP JAMBOREE USA STORY (continued)

Jeep Wrangler TJ on the Rubicon Trail during a Jeep Jamboree.

Terrain will vary on Jeep Jamborees.

TRAIL RATINGS FOR OFF-ROAD ROUTES

Trails are rated from 1 (easiest) to 10 (most difficult). The rating is for the overall trail - not just 1 or 2 rough spots. Rain can increase a trail rating by 2 - 3 points.

Rating 1 - 3:
May not require 4WD. Could be dirt, mud, rocks or other obstacles.

Rating 4 - 7:
Moderate, demanding trails when 4WD is required. Could include boulders, steep hills, and water crossings.

TRAIL RATINGS FOR OFF-ROAD ROUTES (continued)

Rating 8 - 9:
More difficult trails with many obstacles including rock climbing, steep hills, and deep mud. Good chance of getting stuck.

Rating 10:
The toughest. Lots of rock crawling and trails that could cause vehicle damage.

Don't let the trail ratings to intimidate you. It is possible for a driver with a properly equipped 4WD vehicle to start out on higher rated trails. Please note that the higher rated trails have the potential to cause vehicular damage.

TRAINING SPECIAL FORCES - U.S. ARMY
BY MARK A. SMITH OFF-ROADING, INC.

Training Special Forces U.S. Army
in severe off-road driving conditions.

TRAINING SPECIAL FORCES - U.S. ARMY
BY MARK A. SMITH OFF-ROADING, INC. (continued)

LOS ANGELES COUNTY SHERIFF'S TRAINING BY MARK A. SMITH OFF-ROADING, INC.

In 1985, Mark A. Smith, working with Deputy Steve Bellino of the Los Angeles County Sheriff's Department, developed and implemented a special 4WD training program to teach law enforcement officers in the application of 4WD vehicles and equipment. Currently we conduct four courses annually with the Los Angeles County Sheriff's Department. The course is open to all law enforcement agencies throughout the country. We have trained over 3,500 Federal, State and local law enforcement officers throughout the United States. This program is the only certified law enforcement 4WD training in the United States. For additional information on this program, please contact:

Los Angeles County Sheriff's Department
Advanced Training Bureau
11515 South Colima Road, Blg. F103
Whittier, CA 90604
Phone: 562-946-7828
E-mail: mgrichar@lasd.org

"EXPEDICION DE LAS AMERICAS"
CROSSING THE DARIEN GAP

In 1979, Mark A. Smith led an expedition to make a trek from Tierra del Fuego, the southernmost tip of South America, to the icy waters of Prudhoe Bay, Alaska at the top of the North American continent. The "Expedicion de las Americas" required 120 days to complete, and covered over 20,000 miles encompassing the most widely divergent types of terrain and climatic conditions imaginable. By far the most challenging segment of this trip was our traverse of the Darien Gap.

The Darien Gap is an almost incomprehensibly dense 250 mile long stretch of jungles and swamps along the border of Panama and Columbia. Over 400" of annual rainfall in the area creates staggering vegetation growth, making it virtually impossible to cut and maintain even rudimentary foot paths. Fueled by this constant supply of water, certain types of vines in the region have been found to grow at rates of up to three feet per month. There are other hazards to be found in the Darien, as well. Malaria and other tropical diseases are common. Over 100 species of snakes, more than 60 of them poisonous, call the Darien home. Scorpions ranging from half an inch to six inches in length as well as spiders of every size and description are plentiful, as well. Plans show the intended route of the Pan American Highway passing through the Darien, but the sheer difficulty and potential expense of attempting to breach the Darien with paved roads has prevented either government from attempting to complete the project.

The first modern crossing of the Darien was accomplished at a heavy cost by a combined British and Colombian military unit in 1972. 250 British Army soldiers and a compliment of Colombian Marines supported by two vehicles succeeded in crossing the Darien's forbidding terrain in 100 days, however eight of the Marines died during a river crossing along the route.

"EXPEDICION DE LAS AMERICAS"
CROSSING THE DARIEN GAP (continued)

Our Expedicion team consisted of 16 North Americans and three Colombians. Local Choco Indians, sometimes as many as 25, assisted in guiding the group and cutting rough trails with machetes. Five Jeep CJ-7s carried us through the Darien. These unbelievably rugged vehicles were four-speed models equipped with T-18 transmissions, Traclok in the rear differentials, 31" x 10:50 x 15 Goodyear AT tires, Ramsey winches, brush guards and extra skid plates.

Although our Jeeps were incredibly capable vehicles, our Choco Indian friends turned out to be invaluable in devising methods to cross terrain even a CJ-7 couldn't master. Faced with a wide river crossing, the Chocos found and cut down balsa wood trees, floated them downstream to our location and fabricated a raft capable of carrying a Jeep and its crew, all in three hours.

After 30 days, our group emerged safely from the Darien Gap, filled with respect for one of the wildest, most untamed spots on the planet.

"EXPEDICION DE LAS AMERICAS"
CROSSING THE DARIEN GAP (continued)

Obstacles to clear

Typical Jungle - The Darien grows at the rate of 3' per month both from the ground up and the top down

"EXPEDICION DE LAS AMERICAS"
CROSSING THE DARIEN GAP (continued)

Following an Indian foot path

Typical day in the Darien

"EXPEDICION DE LAS AMERICAS"
CROSSING THE DARIEN GAP (continued)

Mud swamps in the Darien

Using two Ramsey winches to help a Jeep up an 85% hill

"EXPEDICION DE LAS AMERICAS"
CROSSING THE DARIEN GAP (continued)

Preparing to winch on a muddy washout

Typical winching situation

"EXPEDICION DE LAS AMERICAS"
CROSSING THE DARIEN GAP (continued)

Using bridging ladders for crossing ravines or climbing steep banks

Winching up a steep incline we named Ramsey Ravine. This involved climbing a slope of up to 85 degrees for over 150'.

SPECIALIZED TRAINING AVAILABLE

Specialized 4WD training is available by some of the most experienced off-road drivers in the world. A training program can be tailored to fit your needs. Corporations, law enforcement, groups and individuals are welcome. Special training in winching is also available.

4WD courses can also be designed and constructed. Mark A. Smith Off-Roading, Inc. has built over one hundred 4WD courses throughout the United States and overseas. We designed and built the 4WD test section at the DaimlerChrysler Proving Grounds in Chelsea, Michigan.

For additional information, please contact:

Mark A. Smith Off-Roading, Inc.
P. O. Box 1601
Georgetown, CA 95634
530-333-4777 x 13 (phone)
530-333-2844 (fax)
pearse@jeepjam.com (e-mail)

HELPING YOU TO ENJOY THE 4WD EXPERIENCE

Jeep®

HELPING YOU TO ENJOY THE 4WD EXPERIENCE

Jeep Jamboree USA
P. O. Box 1601
Georgetown, CA 95634
phone: 530-333-4777
fax: 530-333-2844
e-mail: jeepjam@jeepjam.com
web site: www.jeepjamboreeusa.com

Jeep
web site: www.jeep.com

Goodyear
1144 East Market Street
Akron, OH 44316
e-mail: consumer_relations@goodyear.com
web site: www.goodyeartires.com

Ramsey
P. O. Box 581510
Tulsa, OK 74158-1510
phone: 918-438-2760
fax: 918-438-6688
e-mail: info@ramsey.com
web site: www.ramsey.com

FOR SALE!

ROCK RAILS

For trails rated 4 or higher, on a 1-10 scale, 10 being the toughest, we recommend Rock Rails. We do not recommend Nerf Bars as they cause a loss of clearance. Rock Rails are steel moldings designed to protect your Jeep's rocker panels from rocks, stumps and logs. Steel Rock Rails come predrilled, ready to paint and install with a diagram, photo and instructions. Auto body shops should be able to install them easily. Available for Wranglers, Cherokees, and Grand Cherokees.

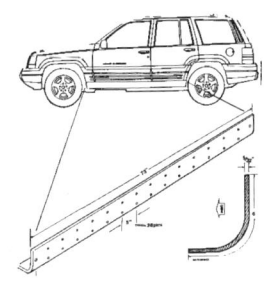

VIDEOS

The World of Four-Wheeling: Bring the fun and adventure of four-wheeling right into your home. Easy-to-learn format provides valuable introduction to four-wheel drive for novices and experienced drivers alike. © 1988.

Expedicion de las Americas: The four-wheel drive adventure of a lifetime; the 120-day, 20,000-mile Jeep trip from Tierra del Fuego to Prudhoe Bay, Alaska via the Darien Gap, the uncompleted portion of the Pan American Highway. The 103 miles of swamps and jungles comprising the Darien Gap required 30 days to traverse. ©1978

DECAL

"It's a JEEP® thing... you wouldn't understand!" (2" x 42")

INSTRUCTIONAL BOOKLET

Mark A. Smith's Guide to Safe, Common-Sense, Off-Road Driving. 82 pages.

For more information, please contact Jeep Jamboree USA
P.O. Box 1601, 2776 Sourdough Flat, Georgetown, CA 95634
530-333-4777 (phone)   530-333-2844 (fax)   jeepjam@jeepjam.com (e-mail)
order ONLINE www.jeepjamboreeusa.com/gear.htm

ORDER FORM

Please allow 2 - 4 weeks for delivery

Quantity	Rock Rails	*Price	Shipping	
_____	Wrangler Model/Year ____	$130.00	$35.00	_____
_____	Cherokee Model/Year ____	$180.00	$35.00	_____
_____	Grand Cherokee 1993 - 1998	$240.00	$35.00	_____
_____	Grand Cherokee 1999 - 2000	$265.00	$35.00	_____
	Videos			
_____	The World of Four Wheeling	$9.95	incl.	_____
_____	Expedicion de las Americas	$17.95	incl.	_____
	Decal			
_____	"It's a Jeep® thing....you wouldn't understand!	$6.00	incl.	_____
	Instructional Booklet			
_____	Mark A. Smith's Guide to Safe, Common Sense Off-Road Driving	$7.95	incl.	_____

Check one: ❏ Visa ❏ MC ❏ American Express
❏ Discover ❏ Money Order ❏ Check
($35 charge for returned checks)

subtotal _____
CA residents add 7.25% sales tax _____
TOTAL _____

BILL TO:

Name: _____

Address: _____

City: _____ State: _____ Zip: _____

Credit Card #: _____ Exp. Date: ___ / ___

Signature: _____

Daytime Phone Number: _____

SHIP TO:

Name: _____

Shipping Address: _____

Mailing Address: _____

City: _____ State: _____ Zip: _____

Jeep Jamboree USA
P.O. Box 1601, 2776 Sourdough Flat, Georgetown, CA 95634
530-333-4777 (phone)   530-333-2844 (fax)   jeepjam@jeepjam.com (e-mail)
order ONLINE www.jeepjamboreeusa.com/gear.htm

(*Current pricing as of March, 2004. Prices subject to change without notice.)

ABOUT THE AUTHOR

Often referred to as "the father of modern four-wheeling", Mark A. Smith shares his decades of experience and innovation to teach the basics of safe, common sense, environmentally conscientious off-highway driving in this handy, glove box sized volume.

In 1953, as a way to attract tourism to their tiny California mountain town, Smith and a group of local boosters began the Jeeper's Jamboree over the Rubicon Trail, an annual trip which would gain such notariety in four-wheeling circles as to become the standard by which all other off-road routes in North America would be judged.

Looking for even greater adventure, in 1979 Smith organized and led the Expedicion de las Americas, a 120-day, 20,000 mile off-road journey from the southernmost tip of South America at Tierra del Fuego to Prudhoe Bay, Alaska, above the Arctic Circle. This incredible trip featured a traverse of the virtually impassable Darien Gap, a 103 mile stretch of dense, hostile jungle which took 30 days to cross.

Seeking a way to share his love of off-roading and the exploration of America's grand back country with the public, Smith founded Jeep Jamboree U.S.A. in 1982. Jeep Jamboree U.S.A. offers guided, family oriented off-road adventures open to any Jeep owner. Over 7,500 Jeep enthusiasts participate in the 35 Jeep Jamborees held each year in locations as diverse as the evergreen forests of Maine and the painted deserts of Utah. This involvement with the Jeep brand brought Smith in closer contact with the manufacturer as well, and since 1982, he has worked as a consultant to the Jeep brand of the DaimlerChrysler Corporation.

In 1986, the United Four Wheel Drive Association recognized Smith's impressive accomplishments, naming him "Four Wheeler of the Decade".

The jungles of Madagascar were the next destination for the globe-trotting Smith as in 1987 he led Camel Trophy in what is perhaps the toughest adventure competition in the world.

ABOUT THE AUTHOR (continued)

Smith's pioneering spirit was next recognized by the exclusive Explorer's Club of New York, which inducted him as a member in 1989.

The off-road prowess of many of America's law-enforcement and military personnel may be attributed to Smith as well. Since beginning off-road training for the Los Angeles County Sheriff's Department in 1984, he has trained over 3,500 law enforcement officers from over 30 agencies, including the Royal Canadian Mounted Police. Ongoing training of the elite of America's military, the U.S. Army Special Forces, continues in remote, sometimes exotic locations as well.

Over 100 off-road demonstration courses have been built by this member of the Off-Road Hall of Fame, including the four-wheel drive test facility at the DaimlerChrysler Proving Grounds at Chelsea, Michigan.

Opinions expressed by the author do not necessarily reflect the views of the persons, corporations or agencies mentioned in this publication.